MW01196159

That Winter the Wolf Came

JULIANA SPAHR

∞

Commune Editions
Oakland, California
communeeditions.com

An imprint of AK Press / AK Press UK
Oakland, California (akpress@akpress.org)
Edinburgh, Scotland (ak@akedin.demon.co.uk)

Cover illustration and Commune Editions design
    by Front Group Design (frontgroupdesign.com)

Library of Congress Cataloging-in-Publication Data

Spahr, Juliana
    That wnter the wolf came / Juliana Spahr

    ISBN 9781934639177 (pbk.: alk. paper)
    Library of Congress Control Number: 2014958777

Printed on acid-free paper by McNaughton & Gunn, Michigan,
    U.S.A. The paper used in this publication meets the minimum re-
    quirements of ANSI/NISO Z39.48-1992 (R2009)(*Permanence of Paper*).

When one fled past, a maniac maid,
And her name was Hope, she said:
                                    — Shelley

TABLE OF CONTENTS

Transitory, Momentary

The Brent geese fly in long low wavering lines on their migrations.
They start in western Europe, fatten in Iceland, then fly over the
Greenland ice cap to Canada. They sometimes breed on the Arctic
coasts of central and western Siberia and winter in western Europe,
some in England, the rest in Germany and France. What I have to
offer here is nothing revolutionary. They learn the map from their
parents, or through culture rather than through genetics. It is just an
observation, a small observation that sometimes art can hold the oil
wars and all that they mean and might yet mean within. Just as
sometimes there are seven stanzas in a song. And just as sometimes
there is a refrain between each stanza. And just as often this sort of
song tells a certain sort of story, one about having something and then
losing it. Just as sometimes the refrain of a song is just one word said
four times. Just as sometimes the word is huge, sometimes coming
from a machine and yet hitting in the heart; uplifting and ironic and
big enough to hold all these things in its four syllables. Just as some-
times, often even, it contradicts, and thus works with, the stanzas. Just
as the police clear out yet another public space and yet another camera
follows along behind. Just as the stream has no narration, only ambient
noise. And the police move slowly, methodically in a line as if they are
a many-legged machine. They know what they are doing. It is their
third time clearing the park and they will clear it many more times and
then they will win and a building will be built where there once was

the park. In this song, as is true of many songs, it is unclear why the singer has lost something, maybe someone. In this time, the time of the oil wars, there are many reasons that singers give for being so lost. Often they are lost because of love. Sometimes they are lost because of drugs. Sometimes they have lost their country and in their heart it feels as if they have lost something big. And then sometimes they are lost just because they are in Bakersfield. Really though they are lost because in this time song holds loss. And this time is a time of loss. The police know, as they move through the park yet one more time, that they will win and a building will be built on the space. But right now, the building is not there. All that is there are the police and debris and the police deal with the debris. They push over bookshelves, open up boxes and look inside, tear into tents, awkwardly, the poles springing. They are there only to see if any humans remain. Tomorrow the bulldozers will push the debris into big piles and load it into trucks. The police wear white helmets and short sleeves under their kevlar vests. For many years the Brent geese ate eelgrass, but once the eelgrass was gone to the wasting disease and the estuaries filled, they moved inland to agricultural lands and began eating grasses and winter-sown cereals. The Brent geese are social, adaptable. They fly around together, learning from each other, even as these groups are often unstable, changing from season to season. Songs in their most popular versions tend to be epiphanic, gorgeous with swelling chord changes, full of lament too. And this song, like many, expresses the desire to be near someone who is now lost. It travels as something layered, infiltrated, unconfused with its refusals to make a simple sense. I want to give you this song sung in a bar in Oakland one night during the ongoing oil wars. The singer had clearly been lost once, but they sang as someone who eventually got in the car and drove out of Bakersfield, perhaps early in the morning, the sun just starting to rise, or perhaps later after sun-up, the light washing out everything in Bakersfield as the sun is wont to do there. Eventually they arrived to sing this song. This might have taken them many years. There was nothing that implied that the lostness was recent. But the lostness, it was clear, was huge and had been experienced fully by them. It probably doesn't matter where the sun was that day in Bakersfield when they got in the car. It probably just matters that there is a sun, still, and they got in the car and drove, drove through the oil fields with their wells pumping out amber colored oils and their refineries with tall towers that heat the oil so as to sort its various viscosities, and drove through the black cloud that is the slow constant burn of the oil wars. Then at some point they were in Oakland. The oil near Bakersfield is heavy but it often benchmarks against the Brent blend. Brent blend is a light crude oil, though not as light as West Texas Intermediate. It contains approximately 0.37% of sulphur, classifying it as sweet crude, yet not as sweet as West Texas Intermediate. When the park is cleared and the building is built, it will headquarter an oil company. When this oil company named their oil fields off the coast of Scotland, they choose the names of water birds in alphabetical order: Auk, Brent, Cormorant, Dunlin, Eider, Fulmar and so on. Brent is also an acronym for the Jurassic Brent formation that makes up the Brent oilfield, for Broom, Rannoch, Etive, Ness, and Tarbert. About two thirds of oil is benchmarked against what is called the Brent Crude Oil Spot price. Petroleum suppliers in Europe, Africa and the Middle East often price their oil according to Brent Crude's value on the Interconti-nential Exchange if it is being sold to the West. The Brent Crude Oil Spot price is set in dollars, maintained by force, endlessly manipulated by commodity futures markets. The refrain is the moment when the singer makes it clear that they understand something about what is being lost. It was obvious they had lost their country, it being taken over by bankers and all. They had clearly been rejected. Loved too much and gotten too little of it back in return, many times. But none of this matters, it was obvious, in comparison to what is now being lost for that night even though the song is about a minor loss, about the loss of tongue on clit or cock, the singer seemed to understand something about the other things that are lost. While a formation of police clear the far side of the park of the debris of its occupation, another forma-tion of police on the other side shoot the new gasses, the ones we do not yet know by name, into another part of the park where people are now clustered. This camera has sound and every few seconds there is a pop. It is unevenly steady. The song is just about two people who are not near each other, who have probably chosen not to be near each

very ironic

The birds are being hurt, but the oil is named after them?

other any more. The song reflects and refracts the oil in ways both relevant and trivial in how it tells about what happens when one lets love go, when one gives up the tongue. It might be that only through the minor we can feel enormity. It might be that there is nothing to epiphany if it does not hint at the moment of sweaty relation larger than the intimate. For what is epiphanic song if it doesn't spill out and over the many that are pulled from intimacies by oil's circulations? The truckers, the sailors and deckhands, the assembly line workers, those who maintain the pipelines, those who drive support in the caravans that escort the tankers, the fertilizers, the thousands of interlocking plastic parts, the workers who move two hundred miles and live in a dorm near a factory, alone, those on the ships who spend fifty weeks circulating with the oil unable to talk to each other because of no shared language and so are left only with two weeks in each year where they can experience the tongue in meaningful conversation. A life that is only circulations. Before the police come, before the building, in the middle of one night, a group of people form a line leading to the entrance of the park. Or several groups form several lines, all leading to the entrance. Some wear medical masks. Some wear glasses too. All pass bricks, one by one, down the line so as to make a pile. They are silent for the most part, silent enough that it is possible to hear the bricks make a clink as they fall. The pile gets bigger and bigger. It is waist high. Then chest high. Some get out of the line and climb on the pile, hold both their hands in the air because they know now is the transitory, momentary triumph and it should be felt. Others continue passing brick after brick, from one hand to another hand, arms extended, torsos at moments also going back and forth with the bricks. When they run out of bricks, the pile is topped with fencing. Then they gather behind it, waiting. Back there, some-one might possibly be singing to a child, singing the epiphanic song that alludes to losing the moment of tongue on clit or cock over and over because the child cannot be comforted, because the singer knows only loss. The room will be dark. The light will be on in the hall. There will be shadows, in other words. And the singer will know about these shadows at this moment and know they had agreed to be with shadows when they had the child. They had gambled in a sense on a question of sustaining. They had agreed to exist from now on with a shadow. A shadow of love and a shadow of the burning of the oil fields that has already happened and is yet to come and yet must come and a million other shadows that might possibly disappear in the light at that moment.

Brent Crude

The Brent Crude Oil Spot price was 101.84, when the first of a series
of meetings are held at a park. I stand at the back during these meet-
ings and hold my son's hand as he jumps in mud puddles after he gets
bored of sitting in the cold. An occupation grows out of these meet-
ings. It feels as if it will never end but really it is only for a few seconds.
Time is weird. One moment I am sitting on a bale of straw in a skirt
and a man rushes over and puts his coat down for us to sit on so I don't
itch my legs and then the next moment I am shopping for particulate
masks on the internet. In between emails of love, pithy and funny
signs, paths made out of pallets, so much music and dancing, my son
rolling his eyes to the back of his head as he dances on stiff legs, lentils
and mac and cheese, poetry readings each week, a man breaking a
piece of wood over someone's head, many tents, photocopied pam-
phlets, layer on top of layer of straw to keep the mud under control,
less pot and fewer murders than usual. I should tell you that I never
spent the night at the occupation. The Brent Crude Oil Spot price is
112.11 when the police come the first time.

Then, the library, walking back, an all night back and forth, tenting
up again, a general strike, a three or so hour building occupation, the
police again, at the library again, walking back again, a port shut down
again, a twelve or so hour occupation of an empty lot, an attempt to oc-
cupy an empty building that fails. O10, O25, N2, N14, N19, D12, J28.

[handwritten margin notes: "sounds normal", "confusing"]

19

I take my son. I do not. I do hold his hand while watching a masked someone break a huge window and I hold it while watching someone throw a chair at a window and I hold it again watching someone paint STRIKE on a window. All the while the Brent Crude Oil Spot price moves from 112.11 down to 106.97 back to 115.61.

I start writing a poem about oil extraction in iambic pentameter because Cara emails me and asks me this: "how can we, as poets, take care of ourselves, our creative work, and the larger planetary body on which we depend?" She wants, she says, to "call attention to the material life of the artist, as person, who, in addition to being creator/conspirator to a body of work, possesses a physical body, and real financial, medical and social needs." I have just finished a collaboration with a friend and I want to get his tongue out of my hand and so I fill my hand with tradition. My collaborator has said to me several times that we don't need another BP poem. The Brent Crude Oil Spot price was 127.85 when we began the collaboration; 112.5 when we ended it.

Around the time I start writing in iambic pentameter, I begin to wear several shirts, a Spanx, the sort that covers the belly but not the breasts, silk long johns, hiking boots, jeans, and a Marmot out on Saturday nights. I have a joke about the Marmot. A sort of are-you-wearing-your-Marmot-tonight joke. This is a joke about being a middle aged body, one whose real medical and financial needs are somewhat met, about to go out and meet some social needs, be with other bodies, bodies whose real medical and financial needs are met variably, some more or less doing ok and some not doing ok at all. Sometimes on these Saturday nights I am part of a group of fifty, sometimes of a hundred. The first time, it is a winter dark night and the light has that yellowish tinge that cell phone cameras are just now beginning to capture. I hear a child chanting as I walk across the plaza, his high voice floating out over the empty space before I see his body, before I see and hear the other bodies. The child's voice is unwavering, strong, and yet eerie as it spills out, amplified. Hey, hey, ho, ho, he says in a high, five year old voice. Fucking police have got to go, a crowd answers. This goes on for some time and then morphs into fuck the police, fuck the police, fuck

20

the police; the child, because he has the megaphone, the loudest. The child saying fuck.

My body is unremarkable, not at all singular, as I walk up to join these other bodies, and it remains unremarkable, not at all singular, as it walks with others, takes off into the street when others do, usually after someone yells block up block up into a megaphone. Then we walk together and yet unevenly out into the street, darkly clad because the facebook invitation said to wear black, in small groups, some faster, some slower, some holding hands, some on bikes, some with canes, sometimes someone in a wheelchair. There is always a megaphone at the front. And then a second later, someone usually on a bike, off to the side, blocking traffic until we cross the intersection. This person calm, smiling.

I have a tendency to anxiously slow down. I also stay to the side. I am nervous, nervous. I want to keep saying this. I am an anxious body. Shortly after we step out into the street, the white vans, which have been idly waiting nearby, pull out and the motorcycles drive up from behind. Engines then and bright directed lights.

We are an awkward formation. Ununited but together. A few carry signs. Some are masked. Some wear a red cross of duct tape. We walk or limp down the street at an awkward pace. The megaphone often tells us to block up, to hurry up, to stay together, stragglers get snatched, stay together so you don't get snatched. Sometimes we scream back, slow down, slow down, there are people at the back. The vans drive slowly behind us. Sometimes there are eight vans. Sometimes three. Sometimes the vans are full. Sometimes not. Those in the vans scramble awkwardly out and stand, bulked, swinging clubs. They have on exoskeletons. They wear their face shields, sometimes pitchers, sometimes catchers. They have video cameras attached to their chests. Some are on; some are off. They carry gas masks at their waist, dangling zip ties off their asses. If things are going to tradition, there is a zone of about three or four yards between these two groups. One group screaming things like Oakland to Greece, fuck the police. Hey

sounds, chaos, people, warnings [handwritten marginal note]

makes me feel like I am in the march [handwritten note]

21

hey ho ho, stop and frisk has got to go or I smell bacon, I see pork, run little piggy, I got fork. Tighten up, says the megaphone.

Once I show up eight minutes late and follow the sounds of chants through the city, around the lake, rushing to catch up. Night herons rest on the concrete edges of the lake, hunting. Teenagers drinking beer sit on the edge, legs dangling. A small group of people in masks run by. I greet two people on a bike who are also late and are now rushing after the chants. Eventually I see vans and motorcycles and I walk through them to join the others. I am glad to be back walking with others.

This sort of walking around the city goes on and on. Week after week. Sometimes I go. Sometimes I stay home. When I go, I often say to myself, how lucky to be outside, out in the night, with friends, walking, despite the vans, the motorcycles, the engines, the lights. I learn the city in a different way.

I wanted to give you a child as a way of thinking about a material life. I said to myself, I will write the child next to the meter, intimacy next to mediation, together next to separation. But I really couldn't figure out why I wanted to give you a child. Is it because a child cannot possibly be an individual creation? Here, a gift, a child, hold its hand. Here. Who wants that?

> 2 people to mak a kid

complex, a whole person

Many recent moments I worry not only my own body but also his body, my mothering. As I held his hand while someone threw a chair at a window, a woman came up and said you and your child should leave; there are black bloc here. Colleagues walked by and yelled, go back, go back. They said, they are vandalizing up there. We kept walking. Then, there I am, a few weeks later, yelling at him, come back, come back. I am trying to pull him away because there is some pepper spray and he is upset with me, wanting to go towards the excitement but as I pull him back I realize I am pulling him back into the motorcycle line. It is raining. We duck into an overhang of a building with a few others. A man named Jesus is there. A few minutes later, a window is broken and I mistake the noise of the broken window for rubber bullets, so I run across the street, out into traffic, dragging my son with me. We run down an alley and then we are out. People going out to dinner walk by. We are then a mother and a son. We have no trouble hailing a cab. We are a family walking with the children's brigade to an abandoned building to share it. The children's brigade is at the back, with prayer flags, songs, and drums. The brigade plans to pull off before we get to the building. I walk too fast with my anxious body again and so we lose the children's brigade. Once we realize, there is a slapstick story of pulling lunches out of a suitcase. I have made the lunch for my son and packed it separately but I have made only one large adult lunch and it has to be split into threes. We are all pulling lunch pieces out of our bags and yelling at each other. Someone is saying mommy I will make you go home if you don't stop. Later we realize that the police at the back didn't keep the zone between the march and themselves. They kept joining the children's brigade and threatening parents with child endangerment.

I do not want to say the children are the future. Ok? But that is just the beginning of what I do not want to say. I do not want to imply that my body is involuntary at these moments. I do not want to suggest an insurrectionary body. I do not want to use the word occupy. I am trying to figure something out. Something I do not yet understand about my physical body, my real financial, medical, and social needs.

all things a child takes away from you

Later that night my son goes home to bed. I wave to him as the car drives off and he waves back. Be safe he is saying out the open car window. I then walk down the street to join the others and fifteen minutes later I am kettled. There is a dispersal order but every time someone tries to disperse there is tear gas. My friend shakes his head and says we are doomed and at that exact same moment a fence is pushed down and someone yells, run, run, and finally, I can anxiously run. Someone holds my hand as I run and before we leave he says run, don't fall and don't stop. I am running and then I am out in the street again, walking with others. A half hour later, I walk out of another kettle. I have been let go provided I do not fail to disperse. I walk out with thirty others, tripping over abandoned spray paint cans, knives, several Gerber multi-tools. We walk out one by one, even if in twos or threes or more. We are not together. We left behind four hundred others. Some of us return to the plaza, not knowing what to do. It has been a long day. We sit on the steps, texting those still in the kettle but not yet cuffed. I find out where keys are and I agree to feed cats, walk dogs, pick up at Santa Rita with a bottle of antacid, Tylenol, strong coffee. Then the door to city hall is open. People rush in. Someone screams they are coming, they are coming. They aren't at that point, but I grab a hand next to me or maybe we grab each other's and then we are off, running across the mud of the plaza, slipping and sliding through it, still holding hands, out into the intersection, the red light is in our favor, down the street, and into a bar. Our material bodies absurd in their nervousness.

There are so many variables in deepwater drilling. The semi-submersible that hovers over the metal casing is kept in place by the constant modulations and adjustments of many position reference sensors, combined with wind sensors, motion sensors, and gyro compasses. These sensors constantly calculate the wind and current drag of the vessel and then control the propellers and thrusters. They give the semi-submersible the illusion of being steady, the amount of steady necessary to tether the casing that extends thousands of feet to the floor of the ocean and then beyond that, into the floor. The cements that line the casing require low viscosities and rapid gel strength development. They must develop compressive strength rapidly at the low temperatures found on the floor of deep oceans. It is this that ensures confident squeeze or no-squeeze decisions. The cement is an art, it is said. No one will release their formulas. Same thing with the drilling mud that is inside the casing. It is the mud that keeps the oil and gas in the casing, releasing it with control. It is full of water, clays, and other chemicals such as bentonite and potassium formate. Sometimes diesel fuel replaces the water. It is also said to be an art, to be owned.

Around the time I start writing in iambic pentameter, someone said
the last thing we need is another BP poem; someone said just another
nature poem; someone said stupid white girls writing about Africa;
someone said I refuse to publish stuff like that. Not to me necessarily.
At other moments to me but that doesn't matter. It was in the air. The
Brent Crude Oil Spot price was 117.18.

If You Were a Bluebird

[handwritten annotations:]
— goes through the elements
— Africa
— building, listing

Began with a list
A bird. Reed cormorant.
Added a fish and a monkey. Hingemouth. White throated monkey.
Added because.
Because the six dorsal and anal fins of the hingemouth and its two
     teeth too and also its swim bladder like a lung, covered in alveoli.
Because the silvery wings, longish tail, and short head crest of the reed
     cormorant.
Because the white throated monkey, with its red belly and its white legs.
Added the phrase the principle of relation.
Because it was with the principle of relation that the Niger Delta came
     to teem.
So the hingemouth with its six dorsal and anal fins and its two teeth
     too and also its swim bladder like a lung, covered in alveoli, swims.
So the silvery wings, longish tail, and short head crest of the reed
     cormorant dives down to considerable depths in the Delta and also
     dives to feed, as it tends to do, in more shallow water, bringing slow-
     moving mormyrids and cichlids to the surface.
So the white throated monkey, with its red belly and its white legs,
     bangs objects against the ground, throws sticks.

Then added another bird.

Eurasian spoonbill.

Added a crab and a fish.

Cleistostoma kuwaitense. Mudskipper.

Again added because.

Because the Eurasian spoonbill with its dark legs, occasionally
grunting and trumpeting.

Because the cleistostoma kuwaitense building a semi-permanent
mud hood over the entrance to its burrow.

Because the mudskipper digging a deep burrow then hiding in it
during high tide, a polygonal territory surrounded by dams, and
defended against rivals, yet also shared with digging crabs.

Added the phrase the principle of relation.

Because it was with the principle of relation that the Kuwait Bay
came to teem.

So the Eurasian spoonbill with its dark legs, grunts and trumpets,
sweeps the end of its partly opened bill from side to side as it
wades through shallow water.

So the mudskipper builds its burrow beneath the mudflats, defends its
territory, keeps a pool of water so as to also engage in surface activity.

So the cleistostoma kuwaitense, using the same mud of these mud
flats, builds a semipermanent mud hood.

— building the
ecosystem of the
Niger Delta

✗ — each place is a
major oil spill

Then another bird.

Pelican.

Added a mammal and a fish. Bottlenose dolphin. Red snapper.

Returned to because.

Because the gregarious pelican, traveling in flocks.

Because the bottle nose dolphin, remembering and comprehending.

Because the nibbling and the picking of the red snapper with its short,
sharp needle-like teeth.

Returned to principle of relation.

Because it was with the principle of relation that the Gulf of Mexico
came to teem.

So the gregarious pelican hunts, hunts cooperatively, plunge dives
from high up so as to stun the fish, scoops them up, and then also
breeds, breeds colonially, in trees, bushes, in the ground, around
the gulf.

So the dolphin talks, talks, over thirty distinguishable sounds.

So the red snapper spreads itself out in the artificial reefs of oil plat-
forms, the smaller fish in the upper part of the water column, the
larger in deeper areas.

I am waiting.
Said this out loud.
Said to no one in particular.   *waiting?*
Said we are waiting.
Some of us are waiting.
Waiting for the assembly of fish.
Waiting to be complete.
Waiting to storm the waters.
Also waiting for the assembly of trees.
Waiting to be complete.
Waiting to be infiltrating the land.
And waiting for the assembly of animals.
Waiting to be complete.
Waiting. Waiting.
Waiting for the assembly of birds.
Waiting to be complete.
Waiting to fly the sky dark.
Waiting for the impossible.
Said waiting.
Meant wanting.
Wanting to fly the sky dark.
Wanting to be complete.

Form change

Wanting the principle of relation.

Wanting for the six dorsal and anal fins of the hingemouth and its two
teeth too and also its swim bladder like a lung covered in alveoli to
be with the red snapper as it nibbles and picks with its short sharp
needle-like teeth to be with the bottlenosed dolphin hunting as it
makes squeaks and whistles and leaps from the water, slaps tail on
the water's surface to be with the reed cormorant as it dives down
into the water with a characteristic half-jump to give itself a more
streamlined entry and then once there under the water propels it-
self with its feet and sometimes with its wings to be with the pelican
as it dives down so as to submerge below the surface, snaps up prey,
surfaces, water spilling from the throat pouch before it swallows to
be with the Eurasian spoonbill as its head moves back and forth as
it holds its bill in the shallow waters of marshes rivers lakes flooded
areas and mangrove swamps deltas estuaries tidal creeks and coastal
lagoons to be with the mudskipper in and out of the water as it is
walks on land too to be with cleistostoma kuwaitense as it builds a
semi-permanent mud hood over the entrance to its burrow to be
with the white throated monkey, cheek pouches full of food.

Wanting to be together.

Hingemouth and red snapper and bottlenosed dolphin and reed cor-
morant and pelican and Eurasian spoonbill and mudskipper and
cleistostoma kuwaitense and white throated monkey and me too. I
mean us. Together.

Together. Water in one hand. The right hand.

Together. Sky in the other. The left hand.

The earth. Together.

Together. Wanting become forests.

Together. Wanting become grasslands.

With the unfeathered legged ostrich and the equal lengthed toed
osprey and the pygmy hippopotamus.

The small things also.

The sulphate reducing bacterias.

The foraminiferal species.

Sandbanks. Swamps. Edges of the open forest.

goes from waiting to wanting

Wanting to be coming to be possibility gathering.
As it happened with blood cockle gathering when the women went to
    gather blood cockles and the cockles were covered in oil.
And then began another sort of gathering.
Gathering so as to be seizing.
Seizing a boat.
Dividing into groups.
Occupying airstrips, helicopter pads, oil storage areas, docks.
Singing all day and night.
Dancing ridicule too.
Chanting of threatening songs.
Attacking of stores and prisons.
Knocking down of telephone poles and severing of wires.
Wearing palm leaves.
Slowly at first.
One at a time.
One location at a time.
And then more.
From four hundred one day to four thousand the next.
Wanting to be coming to be possibility gathering.
As it happened.
The women and the women-identified of 1789 and 1871 and 1917 and
    1918 and 1929 and 1969.
Sometimes they had just a drum and churchbells, then kitchen blades,
    and then suddenly ten thousands.
Sometimes they began with stones and snowballs and then they turned
    to attack police stations.
More.
Always more.
For more.
Like how the white throated monkey does it, five or six at the begin-
    nings, then more gathering up to thirty.
But not stopping then.
Gathering like the silt too.
Traveling through the circuits that already exist.
Traveling with the ease of oil tankers.

From Banias in Syria, Tripoli, Ceyhan in Turkey.
Through the Neutral Zone to the terminals at Mena Saud and Ras Al
　　Khafji.
Through Umm Said.
Through Das Island and Jebel dhanna.
Arjuna, Balongan, and Cinta, and Widuri.

Relationality
　　｜
　　the principle of relation

　　　－ the relationship
　　between each animals,
　　　the world

　　complex interactions

－ The nature is stable until
　　the oil creates
　　an unstable situation

　　the oil companies are
　　unimpacted
　　(causing damage to
　　　　other systems)

Calling You Here

if you were a snowy plover, you'd be surface feeding
if you were a northern pintail, you'd be continually whistling
if you were a magnificent frigate, you'd be flamboyantly displaying
you'd know what you'd need
if you were a laughing gull
or a red-breasted merganser
if you were this moment, this world

if you were a clean long rain
do you think I could stand it?
honey, if you were a clean long rain,
I'd be there within it, I'd be there with you
if you were pristine beaches and salt marshes
extremely wide tidal zone
shallow near shore waters
I'd stretch alongside you
I'd help you pass by ways that had dissatisfied you
I'd be there with you
I'd be there stretching
I'd be there fetching you too

but you are not a clean rain
and you are not pristine
but still we are together extremely wide tidal zone
shallow near shore waters
do you think we can stand it?

if we were a pygmy scaly-tailed flying squirrel, we'd swing down and
    bite them.
if we were an oryx, we'd use our horns against them
if we were an explosive, we'd explode alongside them
if we came together and laid down in a farm land
if we came together and occupied a grassland
if we came together and departed from ways
if we came together our reasons be spreading
our waters, our lands
we'd be calling
we'd be calling you here

Dynamic Positioning

It is dynamic positioning that
Allows a semi-submersible the

Ability to hover there over
The well. It is a thirty-six inch tube,

A casing, that extends down to allow
The drill and bit to be rotated there;

The drill then spudding in; the seafloor, dark,
And giving way. It is a thick column

Of drilling mud that keeps natural gas
And oil beneath the seafloor while the well

Is capped and it is a cement that
Fills in the casing so the drill pipe stays

Unmoving, stable, in this ever moving sea.
It is a sort of drilling mud that is

Then pumped through the drill pipe and out through
The drill bit then up through the casing and

Then back up to the oil rig in the space
Between the drill pipe and the inner wall.

It is a blowout preventer, a series of valves
That seal off the excessive pressure should

The wellhead kick then blowout. There are all
These variables. Various valves. Pressures.

Buoyancies. Mixes of cements. Currents. Claims.
Humans. Bow spring. Top plug. Shoe track. Floatshoe.

I could go on and on here calling the
New muses of innovation, common

Vocabulary, that covers over the
Elaborate simplicity of this,

This well, Macondo well, was drilled by
Deepwater Horizon and it went through

Five thousand feet, through the abyssal zones,
The epipelagic with its sunlight

The mesopelagic with its twilight
The bathypelagic with its midnight

Then where the sea meets floor, the deep ocean,
A blowout preventer there with the fish,

The darker fish, the large detritevars
That feed on the drizzle of the moulted

Exoskeletons, the carnivores, snipe eels
Big lantern fish, and zooplankton, corals.

This well then went on reaching for the oil
Another thirteen thousand feet. When it hits

The pay zone, down through it, down deeper, deep.
This well, Macondo well, was exploratory.

This story then begins with other wells,
But I will tell the story of This Well:

In April twenty ten, the setting south
And east of Louisiana's long coast.

It begins with a round of tests, some done
And some avoided. An environmental

Impact and blowout plan declared to be
Not necessary. Drilling easy. Then

On April twenty, bled off five barrels
Of fluid, reduced drill pressure. No flow.

At noon, a drill pipe goes in hole so as
To begin mud displacement. Seawater

Then pumped in to displace mud. Kill line
Not bled. It goes on like this. Partial lab

Results, a circulation pressure that
Did not yet match the modeling results

And yet cement job pumped. Fluid returns
Observed. Bottom plug ruptured. Still the

Cement is pumped so it bumps top wiper plug
At twelve thirty. Then two pressure tests.

The drill pipe run in hole to eight thousand
And three hundred and sixty seven feet.

So mud displacement starts, the seawater
Is pumped, then the spacer, then the fresh

Water. The kill line opened and pressure then
Decreased. Drill pipe pressure increased.

The kill line shut in. Mud offloading done.
It goes on. Drill pipe pressure. Kill line open.

Then drill pipe pressure high again. Then sea-
Water is pumped. Kill line full. Kill line

Opened, bled to mini trip tank. Flow
Is stopped. Kill line monitored. It

Is then open. No flow. Considered
A good test. Blowout preventer open-

Ed, seawater then pumped down the drill
Pipe to displace the mud and spacer from

The riser. It is nine o'clock. The flow
Out from the well increased. Trip tank then

Emptied. Then fluids discharged overboard. Pumps
Restarted. Drill pipe pressure on constant

Increase. It goes on like this. Pump number
Two started. Pressure spike. Then pumps two, three,

And four are shut down. Pump one still online.
Then pumps three, four restarted. Pressure build-

Ing, pump two. Pumps shut down. First pump three, four,
Then one. Then drill pipe pressure fluctuates.

Increases. Then decreases. Then again
Increases. Then held briefly, then again

Decreases. A repair begins. At some
Moment hydrocarbons enter the bot-

Tom of the well undetected and rise
Inside the wellbore, growing quickly as

They meet the lower pressure of the sur-
Face, heavy drill mud, other fluids, sea-

Water, all pushed by the rising and
Expanding gases followed by more,

By high pressure oil, gases, other flu-
Ids, all there rising, swelling in

The wellbore, all there, pushing from the
Reservoir. It is almost at ten

O'clock when mud begins its overflow-
Ing of the line and then on the rig floor.

It is almost at ten o'clock when mud
Then shoots up through the derrick. It is almost

At ten o'clock, diverter shut so that
The gas and drilling fluid could be routed

To the baffle plates, the poorboy degass-
Er, then the lower annual prev-

Enter is activated. The drill press-
Ure, the volumes of gases, fluids, drill-

Ing mud, seawater, then is steadily in-
Creasing. And it begins again. Or be-

Gins some more. First as mud. A mud that roar-
Ing, rained. Then the gas as it discharge-

Ing, hissing, the poorboy degasser fill-
Ing. Next the first gas alarm then the oth-

Ers. It was then almost close to ten o'
Clock, still when next a roaring noise, a vib-

Ration, engines began rapid increase-
Ing as also the drill pipe pressure rap-

Idly increasing as the rig then los-
Ing power, shut down processes then fail-

Ing. First explosion on five seconds aft-
Er. Then explosion again, ten sec-

Onds later. It was not yet ten
O'clock when the mayday call was first made.

The Deepwater Horizon gutted stem
To stern. What happens next ends with eleven

Dead. The rig tethered still to the deepwell.
The shrapnel. The lightbulbs then popping. The

Heat. Hot fireballs. The lifeboats smoke filled ovens.
Some lifeboats left, not yet full. Those left

Behind then jumped in to oil-covered,
Still water and so swam away. Some died:

Jason Anderson. Bubba Burkeen. Shane
M. Roshto. Donald Clark. Wyatt Kemp. Karl

Dale Kleppinger. Gordon Lewis Jones. Keith
Blair Manuel. Dewey Revette. Adam

Weise. Stephen Ray Curtis. I will not tell
You their lives, their loves, their young children, their

Relationship to oil. Our oil. The well
Exploded. They then died. Some swam away.

Some floated away in boats. Donald Vidrine,
Curt Kuchta, Jimmy Wayne Harrell. I did

Not die. I watched it then burn on a
Flat screen. Anthony Brian Hayward, Steven

L. Newman, David Lesar watched. And
Susan Birnbaum too, watching.

Tradition

I hold out my hand.
I hand over
and I pass on.
I hold out my hand.
I hold out my hand.
I hand over
and I pass on.
Some call this mothering,
this way I begin each day by holding out my hand and then all day
    long pass on.
Some call this caretaking,
this way all day and all night long, I hold out my hand and take engine
    oil additive into me and then I pass on this engine oil additive to
    this other thing that once was me, this not really me.
This soothing obligation
This love.
This hand over
and this pass on.
This part of me and this not really me.
This me and engine oil additive.
This me and not really me and engine oil additive.
Back and forth.

All day long, like a lion I lie where I will with not really me
and I bestow upon not really me
refractive index testing oils and wood preservatives.
I lie with not really me all day long,
and so I bequeath not really me a honeyed wine of flame retardants
    and fire preventing agents.
I make a milk like nectar,
a honeyed nectar of capacitor dielectrics, dyes, and electrical insulation
and I pass it on every two hours to not really me.
Not really me is a ram perched on a cliff above a stream,
unable to be quenched by the flame retardant in furniture.
Not really me comes near
and takes a nectar of insulated pipes, and some industrial paints.
Later I pass the breast cup to not really me,
a breast cup filled with sound insulation panels and imitation wood
    with a little nectar and sweetness.
And not really me drinks it and then complains a little,
rebuking me, for my cakes of nuts and raisins
are cakes of extraction of crude petroleum and natural gas,
for my apples are filled with televisions and windshield wiper blades.
On my breast are the curls of not really me
and against the brow of not really me wafts plasticizer used in heat
    transfer systems.
As drinking not really me takes in anger and in need
not really me drinks from the hand of that sweetest sleep the juice of me
that cup of adhesives,
that cup of fire retardants,
of pesticide extenders.
And as not really me drinks
I cradle the moon and not really me in my right hand
my lips kissing with the dedusting agents and wax extenders.
Then later in the night,
the bed scattered with the stains of cutting oils and gas-transmission
    turbines,
the blankets with blends of hydraulic fluid,
we lie there together

handing over and passing on
filled up and attempting to think our way through
economics and labor and time and biology
me and not really me
together.

I'd like to think we had agreed upon this together,
that we had a tradition,
that we agreed these things explained us to us
but when not really me wakes
after drinking the pharmaceuticals and photo chemicals
night after night
and day after day
not really me will sing a song of rebuke,
sing the song of not really me, the song that
goes like Salutations to brominated fire retardants of Koppers Ind.
goes like Salutations to water/oil repellent paper coating of 3M
goes like Salutations to wiper blades of Asahi
goes like Salutations to bike chain lubricant of Clariant International
goes like Salutations to wire and cable insulation of Daikin
goes like Salutations to pharmaceutical packaging of DuPont
goes like Salutations to nail polish of Dyneon
goes like Salutations to engine oil additive of Agrevo E
goes like Salutations to hair curling and straightening of Agsin Ptd. Ltd.
goes like Salutations to insecticide and termiticide for empty green-
    houses of Chevron Chemical
goes like Salutations to greenhouse flowers of Monsanto
goes like Salutations to insecticide to kill fire ants of Rigo Co.
goes like Salutations to plasticizers of US Borax Inc.
Not really me's song will go on and on.
Not really me will sing it all night long
hour after hour for weeks on end.
It will have eighty-five company names in it.
It will have twenty-one chemical functions in it.
It will have ninety-seven products in it.
It will have two hundred trade names in it.

Not really me's song will rotate through these names in all their
    combinations.
And then it will end with another part that is as long as the first and
    inventories the chemicals that not really me does not yet know.
But oh those of you who are not really me at all
I say let wisdom be your anvil and knowledge your hammer.
Hand this over.
Pass this on.

Went Looking and Found Coyotes

And there we were.

The light that fall was somewhat golden.

The trees held their leaves for longer than usual and it was warm in a cool sort of way.

There was a mist or a fog or a smoke that held us

And we walked with this mist or fog or smoke and amidst it also and we breathed it in, deep.

It cloaked us. From the inside.

That winter the wolf came.

Came to us. Came near to us. Walked toward this fog of us.

He was two and a half years old and he was the first one back.

He was alone. Wandering over mountains. Across highways. Through forests.

Back and forth he went. Alone.

He was looking for others.

They were not to be found.

Yet he was mutual, we noticed, he cavorted with coyotes.

What else could he do?

He was the only one, not as in the chosen one, but as one of the un-
eradicated ones.

We called him OR7.

That winter, as OR7 walked to where we were, although not with any
desire to be with us,

we waited for the mist, the fog, the smoke to turn into the rains,

saying to each other often that the rains are coming, surely the rains
are coming.

But the rains never really came.

Or came so late that we barely noticed them.

When they arrived, we just put up a tarp and waited them out.

Together. There. Under the tarp. For a few minutes. Unevenly, there.
But there. Together. Still.

That tarp is a version of what mattered. Together.

That winter, we were mainly men.

Not at first, but later,

At first, it was hard to say.

We were so many different things.

That was the idea.

By the end though, by winter, we were mainly men.

And those of us who were not men circled around each other
unevenly.

Still learning though. Still. Together. We had no other choice.

That winter every time we wrote the word "interest" we replaced it
with the word "love."

That winter we just rhymed and rhymed on. Together. Using words.
Together. That winter everything suddenly written in our pentame-
ters, our alexandrines, our heroic couplets, which was often an asso-
ciational sentence-based quiet line, one indebted to lyric in which
the we stood in for the beloved and yet there was almost never a
description of this beloved, no listing of their red lips, their firm
breasts, their smooth skin, leaving a sort of generic atmosphere.

I could tell you of the other things too.

A European influence.

A Middle Eastern influence.

A list of skirmishes.

A feeling of it being nothing. No wait, something. No see, nothing.
    Possibly something. No. Nothing.

Let's just admit it.

We lost all the skirmishes, even the one called the PR war.

But that winter, we were there.

Under a tarp. Close. Together

Just dealing with. Together. Went looking and found coyotes.

It's All Good,
It's All Fucked

It's all good, I would say, it's all fucked. And then I would breathe.
And then, again, it's all good, it's all fucked. Again, breathe. And
then, it's all good, it's all fucked. Breathe again. I might do this while
walking. Or while driving in the car. Or while lying down, before
taking a nap.

It was Non-Revolution. Or it was me. Or it was Non-Revolution and
me. I was unsure what it really was. Maybe it was my thoughts. My
thoughts at one minute about Non-Revolution. About the smell of
Non-Revolution. Sweat, urine, sage, pot, rotting food, hay, all mixed
together. Perhaps about Non-Revolution's body. I am sure I am not the
only one who has thought it exceptional, but I am also just as sure that
by the standards of bodies, Non-Revolution's is fine but not exceptional.
That is the point. That is why Non-Revolution is called Non-Revolution,
why they have revolution as a possibility in their name but it is a
modified and thus negated possibility so as to suggest they are possibly
neither good nor fucked. Still something about Non-Revolution's smell
and body had gotten into me. It was thin except when it was not. And
not slight except when it was. It had this odd patch of hair on its lower
back. Except when it didn't. And it tasted slightly sour, off. Except
when it was sweet, on. At any moment though, to me, it was like some-
thing so excellent I could not get enough of it.

I will not go on. I do not need to. You know desire's perceptual alterations as well as me, the way that what might repulse someone not going around saying it's all good, it's all fucked might become the very thing that makes someone else go around saying it's all good, it's all fucked. I remember saying to Non-revolution once, after I said I so want to fuck you right now, I said, you smell good to me. These are the mundane things one says in these moments, the moments when one cannot say you smell like sweat, urine, sage, pot, rotting food, hay and it is all good to me in this moment. All I could say was I want to fuck you and you smell good to me.

Our relation was brief. We spent some time together. A few months. Maybe. Perhaps just a few weeks. Depends on how you count it. It happened. It was all fucked. Tongue and hands on clit or cock. Fist fights too. Miscommunication. Constant emergencies. It unhappened. Text after text. Then it happened again. Tongue and hands. Also injuries. Illnesses. More miscommunication. Status updates. Deep emotional confusion. It was all good. Hand in hand. Exuberant, giggling desire. Then it unhappened again. And still, joy. Laughter. Care. Almost psychedelic. A feeling that at moments hinted at rivers running backwards. A flooding in other words. Wind and rain and hatred of capitalism with tongue on tongue. Stuff like that. Happening. All fucked. Unhappening. All good. And also, happening. All good. Unhappening. All fucked. And during these moments of happening, of compassion and dedication, giggling exuberance, hands around waist, turning around and pushing into the wall for the deep moment of tongue against tongue, Non-Revolution was an uneven lover. At moments there. At other moments not. Often Non-Revolution was off with others. Tongue somewhere else in the corner of some other plaza somewhere. This hurt me and it didn't hurt me. I was jealous. I'll admit it. I wanted all of the possibility of revolution all the fucking time. I was willing to take it modified and negated even. But I was not jealous in the convention. I was jealous that I was not there with the exuberance at every moment. I wanted to be. I wanted to be there. I wanted to be there all the time, to be inside every moment, to always be on the lips of Non-Revolution and whomever Non-Revolution was touching with their tongue, whatever parts of bodies of Mexico City, Santiago, El Alto, Madrid, Cairo, Suez, Istanbul, Yenagoa. I wanted to be everywhere that Non-Revolution was. I wanted to be with Non-Revolution and everyone Non-Revolution was with.

I was so classic, so clichéd those months. I joined all the social media and then I checked all the social media I had just joined all the time. I got up each morning just to check my phone, click its button to light it up to see if anyone had texted while I was sleeping. And then, still holding my phone, not yet dressed, uncombed and unbrushed, I would click to check my email. Always looking for Non-Revolution, looking for the white and pink mists of the gases, the burning bus and the burning car too, Non-Revolution wearing a traffic cone hat throwing rocks at the cops as they retreat, the ice pick and the car tires, the hammer and the window, the chair flying through the air, the paint bomb on the visor. And then after that, if nothing was doing, I would calm down, eat breakfast, realize I had not missed something during the night that I did not want to miss. Then after breakfast, I would one by one go through the social media looking for Non-Revolution in the status updates and photos and links of friends and friends of friends. And I often felt a tingling excitement when I found Non-Revolution in the feeds of friends of friends. Non-Revolution in these moments often looked happy, looked a lover, a little drunk, a little stimulated too, a little sweaty, flushed.

I so wanted to be with Non-Revolution, I even went to the assemblies, wanted to be at the assemblies, even though they were often long and it was often cold and I was often sitting outside on concrete, shivering up from the butt. I wanted to be with. I could not drag myself away. At moments this desire made sense. I mean is it not a universal desire to be with under a light urban night sky? With a crowd that moves from annoyance at the man who keeps interrupting to yell I love Michael Jackson to be with this man as we all begin to call out I love Michael Jackson one by one and then the sound guy puts on Smooth Criminal and everyone then rushes the stage, dancing hard? At other moments, off the pigs, a history so rich, so failed, so sad, and yet still so resis-

tant. There, sing-chanting no more pigs in our community which is
followed by the hard beat of off the pigs. And then the pigs are there
coming, of course, and Non-Revolution is texting me. Non-Revolution
is high above me in a building, talking with lawyers about Non-Revo-
lution who got arrested earlier, beaten, and taken to the hospital. Non-
Revolution can see more police gathering behind the ones to whom
we are again sing-chanting no more pigs in our community. Leave,
Non-Revolution texts. Leave, now. And I am so caught in the moment,
I can't leave. I can't stop the hard beat chanting of off the pigs with.
Then more police come around the corner, some of them rushing in
to grab us, part of the crowd screaming, part of it trying to pull back
those who are getting snatched, part of it running like gazelles towards
me, and I run ahead of them, with them and away from them to get
out of their way. Then suddenly police running towards me and us and
then I am running with in between the police, their line is not holding,
and I see Non-Revolution running down the street beside me and I say
hey and nothing else as we run together, grabbing each others hands,
and run down the street, into the bar. Again.

During these weeks, these months, Non-Revolution was a particularly
cloudy and confused meme. Like wind and rain and rivers running
backwards. I had no control. When I wondered it, wondered how
it could be like this for me at this moment, I blamed it on the art.
For all the art I have ever loved has been for whatever it is that Non-
Revolution was suggesting it could possibly be. For the river running
backwards. For the wind and the rain. And I am someone who loves
art, who has always loved art, despite. Despite its institutions and its
patronages and its nationalisms and its capitalisms. All the art that has
had a crowd scene in it in which the crowd has been loved, I have
loved. The moment in realist painting of the riot when the perspec-
tive switches from the soldiers' point of view to that of the crowd and
the people in the crowd are individuals flowing over and out of the
space in the painting and the dog is barking causing a horse to rear up
and the soldiers in the crowd are at risk, isolated from the rest of the
soldiers who are off there far in the distance, and one of the rioters in
the crowd has a spy glass trained on these soldiers so they are far off

and the crowd seems to be having fun, even the dog joining in, things tumbling. The crowd in this moment. Complicated, but still joyous, transitory, momentary, experiencing this one moment of freedom before what we know is to come because we know history and we know the crowd will not win. Just one day I noticed this, and I should say that I was able to notice this because I had sing-chanted with, from then on, a different sort of art. All art either with the crowd or with the police. All art coming down to that simple divide.

When I was off doing non-revolutionary things, such as drinking the whites newly arrived from Croatia with the poets or eating the thinly sliced cured meats at the bar with the historian of revolution who disdained Non-Revolution, I kept thinking about wanting to be with instead. At moments I would give myself over. I would just get up and leave, leave the historian of revolution who kept pressing his leg against mine while mocking my attraction to Non-Revolution, and walk out of the bar and down the street to the plaza to be with. And when I got to with, it was entirely possible, likely even, that Smooth Criminal was playing and a form of dancing that made no sense was going on, messy, chaotic, slightly frightening in its uneven physicality and very likely at that moment the sky was a deep, dark clear, with no stars because of the lights on the buildings. There jostled in that crowd by the felonious and the thieving and the sincere and the opposition-ally defiant and the stoned and the overeducated and underemployed and the constantly shaking and the drunk all the time and the missing teeth and the bloodstained crescendo Annie and even by the socialist with the small yapping dog, at that moment I would feel I had made a right decision. Were we okay? Like Annie, of course we were not, would not ever be because we were Non-Revolution. We were with instead. But not just any old sort of with, but with each other in the hatred of capital-ism. And if I was a poet of many centuries previous, I'd call that the sweet-est wine of the beloved.

When I say Non-Revolution and a river running backwards, it was not that the ground rippled and quivered. Not that chasms opened up. Not that sand and dirt exploded from the ground like volcanic eruptions and blotted out the sun as the water ran backwards and boats were dragged upstream. Not that. It was more like there was a river that led into a lake and then there was a long drought and as the water dried up, the lake began to slowly seep out into the river. This was how the river ran backwards. Slowly, in a small way, incrementally, over time. Still it was a time when a river ran backwards and those times are rare enough that I felt lucky to be able to say the river ran backwards or the river is running backwards, lucky to notice it and put my hands into it and feel it running backwards, wet, cool.

It was all good and it was all fucked while it lasted. But eventually Non-Revolution and me were over. It was not that one day I woke up and knew it was over. What we had, Non-Revolution and me, was like all relationships, built to last. But unlike many relationships, everything was against us. Yes, we cared for each other. Yes, we learned to tend to each other's wounds too, to medicate and to bandage. But we suffered from a larger social lack of care or worse a relentless disdain. We were together but we were in it alone at the same time. Except the state was there with us in all sorts of ways. And we suffered from too much of a different sort of care from the state. And we knew history. We knew we would not be together long.

But still long after it was clear it was over we kept texting. Kept emailing. I continued looking through the feeds of friends of friends for Non-Revolution, clicking like when I found them. At first everything was just less. The texting had less joking. Less innuendo. Less love. The images were less triumphant. Benefits, BBQs, squats. Then the rains came and after that the snows and then the rivers filled up and they fed into the lake and the lake filled up slowly and the river no longer ran backwards. And all at once the social media feeds filled up with poets who got Shirley Manson as their alt-rock grrrl, newly bathed and trimmed little dogs, cats with moustaches, babies in funny hats. I still got up each morning and looked for Non-Revolution in the feeds of friends and friends of friends but I noticed they looked less often like a lover. More often they looked tired and run down. They were starting a social center or a school of some sort or assembling an anthology for a revolutionary theory reading group. They were building out walls, hammers in their hands, attempting to build a plaza within. I knew this happens. The move from Non-Revolution with its minor insurrections to social center. I knew going into it that it never lasts with Non-Revolution. I never thought it would. I just knew I wanted it in whatever moment I could get it. If it did not end, if it became Revolution, I knew that would be hard. That was an entirely different lover, one I was not sure I was ready for and yet longed for so much that they often showed up in my dreams and led me by a hand into an incredible sadness and a high so intense that the personal sadness would become incidental to the possibility. I mean I will take that hand and be lead to whatever room when it comes because oh my god, the body of Revolution is something magnificent. But I also know that at that moment I will know the meaning of it's all fucked so hard. And yet still, that hand and the body attached to it. There is no not taking it.

One day, thinking my obsessive thoughts about Non-Revolution, I walk into a coffee shop and sit down before my computer. By one day I mean today. I mean right now. This is where I am now, writing this story of the most minor of uprisings. A story about how when I entered into this one for a brief period of time I agreed to experience all the emotions and I realized that there was a good chance that one of them would be sadness. Minor sadness, I had hoped. What I have now, even though minor, is a sadness that has made it hard for me to concentrate. The coffee shop is full of light and tables and there is a milky sort of air and I am drinking a coffee that has a smoothness to it that coffee just now is beginning to have. I am writing about the sadness that came over me, over us. But not just sadness. Melancholy. Nostalgia. Anger too. Frustration. Bitterness. I do not know why I want to write this but I feel as if it is something I have to do. I write about who this us could possibly be. If it could possibly be. About how I am still texting with Non-Revolution about missing the Non-Revolution. I write about the last year. The dissolution. I write about the social centers. About being the only woman for a while in the revolutionary theory reading group until I wasn't and it was mainly women. About the possible snitches and disrupters, about who got paid by the state for that work and who just idiotically did it for free. I write about the drugs, those we sold and those we bought and what both these acts did to us, did for us. And I write about the fights we have had among ourselves over the last year. Because we have fought hard. About how we perform these fights for each other with our teeth showing a little and the fights from the outside might have looked like the end of any us but to us the fights felt familiar and we fought with our teeth a little but also with our hearts in our hands to get back to life, to refuse to die, to just feel. We fought because we became through fight. And because we don't agree and because we cared with an intensity. I am unsure of my metaphors. Were we wolves? Were we even we? Were we lovers or were we just a brief hook up? Was Non-Revolution the hard dancing one sometimes does to feel less middle aged? Does it even matter?

As I am writing this absurdly specific and muddled story that I am knowing I will be deleting in the near future, I am also listening to a woman who is talking loudly at the table beside me. She is talking to an old friend she has not seen for years, a friend who had been in a moment with her. She is telling a story similar to the one I am trying to tell but of ten, fifteen years previous. She talks about the moment when she went to go meet what she thought would be two hundred people and when she got there three thousand people were there. And then she knew something was kicking off. As she tells it, she is off and running, the months after that are a blur of tearing apart the police barricades and burning them in the bonfire, warming her hands on various fires, marshmallows too, running around a corner into a police line, accidentally, the person beside her screaming who made this route?, who made this route?, then on the other side, blood pouring out of a jaw, a head, an arm, in a nun's habit, running down the street, gaining volition so as to put the ice pick into the sidewall, barely stopping to pull it out with a twist, unarresting a friend, pulling on her arm until the friend twists free, and they go tumbling, together, police running after her, their clubs raised, a dog running beside her yapping, yapping, later in jail, getting a 104 degree fever and being taken off to the sick ward, lost for days. She is talking about the moment when she felt something. She was there. She was there with. And she can't stop talking about it. It is clear that she has lost something and she barely holds onto it and she can't find it again and this is a loss.

I turn back to my writing. I am unsure what I think about her story. It moves me. I identify with her sadness that her Non-Revolution is gone but I am also wondering why was she not with me in the last few years. What kept her away from being with, being with me? I wanted her as I wanted everyone. When I resurface, she is talking about meeting her partner. And how when she saw her she tried to kiss her right away and the partner turned her head and said not yet and everyone in the bar laughed at her but she said she knew then, she knew something about being awake and she would be awake with this woman. This moment too. Then about her son being born, the moment when his heart began to beat and the body filled with the oxygen and the blood turned red and then there was the scream and the scream would be the scream for years to come. He is still screaming she said and I knew what she meant too. That moment. With. With. With. I am listening to her and I am with her. She knows something, how this being with can be easily described with the private emotions of love and desire, the same emotions that are pillaged and packaged in popular music. This is the language she has, a language given to her by multinational corporations. A language of idealized family. I realize it might not be your language. You might have your heroic moments, your bromantic odes of insurrection. Those too.

And yet as she talks, I am listening and I am writing. And as she talks about her own specific story, I am thinking about how she is saying something about how there are not that many possible loves. When I say that I am not saying something about humans. I do not mean actual lovers. There are endless possible lovers. There are more than seven billion possible lovers most days. The categories of love, how- ever, are multiple and yet also limited. When I decided to have a child I said I wanted to have a child because I wanted to experience all the loves. I had experienced many loves of the limited possible loves. I had loved many ways too. I had put parts of my body inside other bodies and let other bodies enter mine. And I had not done this and I had still

loved with an intensity. Variously. I inventoried these loves sometimes.
Some of them I liked. Some of them I didn't. But I studied these loves
and I coveted them and I held onto them and I respected them. But
before I had a child, I had not yet known the love of growing another
body inside my body. And I had not yet known the love of letting that
body come out and go off into the world. And after that, I needed to
also learn to love the toddler who takes off, loving the moment when
love runs away and from the running gets both attention and freedom
from attention, gets being alive and gets this will go on, gets to know
that this running towards and running away will be life in its best mo-
ments, because it feels so good, so now, so full of every best moment
yet to come. Before I just knew running. The love of running. I did not
yet know the love of the lover of running. But after, I learned to love
the lover of running. I am writing that down. I am writing this down. I
am not happy with any of it. I turn off my computer with annoyance.
I finish my coffee. And I leave. I walk out into a warm late afternoon,
leaves still on the trees but not for long, sun at a slant, and go to meet
a friend.

My friend waits for me on a nearby corner. We hug, decide to get
dinner in a bar. We eat fried fish. Drink dark beers. There is also a
coleslaw that is heavy on mayonnaise. The beer cuts the grease in my
mouth and I am glad to have it. The bar is warm, vibrant, feels as if it
has been there for years but I know it is new, fake, and I don't really
care. We talk about Non-Revolution. About how they are. About where
they might be now. Will they come back? What is left of them? My
friend is years younger than me and more experienced too. She thinks
of the last few years as life, not as a lover she met on the street and
took up with briefly. She has been in and out of jail. House arrested
too. She has blockaded several ports. I tell her as we talk about how
so many of the poets that I know, many of them poets that I love in
a certain complicated way, are writing about their hesitations about
being with Non-Revolution. I have a long list of poems, books of
poems, prose too, blog posts, status updates, interviews, conversations
at parties. I tell her how I am abandoning the mantra of it's all good,
it's all fucked and now I just walk around muttering fuck all y'all. I am

sensitive, I told her. They are hurting me, I told her. They keep writing justifications about how they refused to throw down with Non-Revolution. They mention Non-Revolution's bad aesthetics, their awkward dancing, their bad teeth, the way they were always stoned, or easy, or a mess. Too skinny, they say. Hair on back, as if that was a meaningful insult. Smelly maybe too. Like sweat, urine, sage, pot, rotting food, hay, all mixed together. Or sometimes it was about them. Because they were in a break up. Because they were in a relationship. Because they had a young child. Because they liked wine, especially French ones. Because it made them feel awkward. Because Bifo told them it was okay not to. Because they were writers and they wrote FTP, they didn't have to sing-chant with an anti-capitalist crowd. Because they donated on kickstarter instead. Or they watched the livestream. And I couldn't stop reading their accounts and then on top of them, I told her, I was feeling both rejected by Non-Revolution who never texted anymore, not even FTP, and then trivial for falling in love with such a minor uprising, for taking a brief hook up so seriously, for feeling so sad. And there I would be reading, listening, and yet at same time petulantly going fuck all y'all, and then I would say to myself that at least I had once said to Non-Revolution I so want to fuck you and I meant it. At least I knew that moment. At least I knew something about the sour and the sweet, about the smell of sweat, urine, sage, pot, rotting food, hay, all mixed together, running down the street, holding hands. And come on, that moment. That moment. Sometimes one goes one's entire life thinking one will show up for that moment if it just came and it never comes. It is not like any one individual gets to call it into existence. It comes to you as it comes to others, slowly building and then suddenly there, comes as a sort of lucky. And a version of it came to me, an imperfect version, but still I let all its minorness into me. And now I was something running backwards, something unable to be writing, something nostalgic.

My friend looks at me and she says what is wrong with you? and I say nothing, I'm just confused. And then she says I was worried you were choking; you had a funny expression. Her question was literal. But it's like that. A sort of choking. A staring off into space that often precedes a coughing-choking. The it of it's all good, it's all fucked. The depression that follows after the most mundane of uprisings is over. Life feels less. And might for a long time. It might be years before a day will go by that I do not think about Non-Revolution. Wonder where they are. Wonder what they are doing. Want them back in my social media feeds. Want them to text me from the plaza, the park, the statue saying we are here, come down. Want them to say it is kicking off or throwing down in the coded way one has to use in the time of the NSA, something that says bring your tools and your masks and your vinegars, something that says FTP.

My friend goes on. She makes a joke about poets and kickstarters, a joke about poets having money. And god bless them she adds. She is trying to cheer me up and yet trying also to respect me. This respect thing is taking some work on her part. I can tell that it is puzzling my friend that I have held onto every possible turn of phrase ever said by a poet and read it as critique, as mattering in some way. She has read nothing of what I am talking about. She doesn't even know the poets really. She does not understand why it matters to me. I know she finds art at best trivial, at worst capitalist. And I also know she appreciates that when there is a kickstarter, it is often the poets who donate. But still she says the obvious things that any friend would say to someone who first goes around muttering it's all good, it's all fucked and who now goes around muttering fuck all y'all. She begins by saying something about how I had it all wrong, how it's more like people are writing heroic stories in which they write themselves into Non-revolution's advances and say their way of loving is loving Non-revolution. But she gets it, she gets that I am there going no, they didn't, they didn't love Non-Revolution like I loved Non-Revolution. Maybe they didn't put their hands in the water when it ran backwards, didn't feel that moment. And yet, she continues, they loved and might have even made out, maybe even fucked Non-Revolution. Maybe you see it as without your intensity but, she continued, why not have some compassion for those who according to you missed out? You put your hands in the water and the backwards water was something you had not felt before and it made you moist and now the water goes forward as it always has. I get it, she says, relationships I have been in have ended and I too have felt sad about this. But, she says next, why the resentment? Is it really that terrible to see someone claim to have loved a lover that you have also loved?

We have several more beers and we continue talking and she is gener-ous to me and at some moment she says you can still think of yourself as pretty despite it all and I start to cry because she has realized some-thing about how I am trivial and then we realize we have to leave. She has to go to work. I will go home to read. We hug on the street corner. I watch her walk off, confident, with many years of walking off ahead of her. I stand on the corner for a few minutes feeling lost, with a funny almost choking expression on my face. I decide to walk home. It will take an hour but it will let me find myself. I get out my phone. I don't bother to check my feeds. I know nothing is throwing down near me. I am, after all, standing on the corner of 14th and Broadway, so I would know it if something was. Instead I put on my earphones and click on the app that imitates the radio. A country song about abandonment is playing, about laying down on the bathroom floor, about wasting all those tears. The song is simple in its structure. Three chords, of course. Two four line stanzas and one half stanza. An extended ten line re-frain. The refrain repeats once after the first stanza and then twice after the second stanza. The song begins and ends with the singer crying on the bathroom floor but the song resolves it too. I'm through with all the crying the song states, even though the song gets all its power from being about the soft crying after being left standing on the street corner. I begin walking, determined, head down.

Turnt

Sometimes it feels like it is over and it's not.
Sometimes it feels like it has just begun and it's over.

It's dark often at these times.
Urban though, so a certain version of light too.
It's hard to predict if it will start on time or how late.
I'm often a little late and it has started. Last night, I could tell from the
    copters overhead that I was late.
As I walked up, the blocks around it were emptying out.
Parents pulled their children home.
The night herons settled into trees.
That's the outer ring.
As I got closer, all that was left were the blinking lights of the motor-
    cycles blocking the intersections and the men and few women in
    uniforms that mill about the corner, helmets in their hands. They
    talked among themselves. Ignored me mainly. One told me how to
    get around. I did not clarify that I was walking towards.
You can hear it sometimes. It often has a soundtrack. Sometimes it has
    drums and brass. Sometimes just joy.
When I am late I am trying to guess its path. Last night, several times I
    got close to it only to be turned back by a line of cops.

They let the media through but turned me back.

Then it turned the corner and there it was.

At that moment, I melted my body into it and it embraced me.

Rosy fingered dusk and all that.

Come here, it sang, listen.

And then I was borne along by the waves all night and the whirlpool,
    the fig tree, and I was the bat, hanging on patiently.

Aarav came up and hugged me.

Someone grabbed me from behind and I thought it is Artem but later
    realized it was Berat. So much mask.

I grabbed Charlotte's hand and held it for a while when things felt
    dicey.

It felt dicey as they cornered us from two sides and we went down the
    tight side street, up the hill. Charlotte's hand.

It's like that.

Moving from isolation to the depths of friends.

At first we didn't mask up. We were poets.

Then slowly one by one we did.

As we got turnt.

As I got turnt I mean.

Sometimes I still don't mask up. It often feels hubristic.

I keep a bandana in my pocket.

It isn't super effective. It falls down a lot.

Last night, I tied it around my neck as we walked up the side street hill.
    I pulled it over my face as I walked past the line of cops. I noticed
    Emma there, throwing eggs. I ducked. Two balloons filled with
    paint flew by. Visors suddenly yellow.

She said to me, how is your heart?

And I at first worried her question.

Then I realized she meant my heart and how it was turnt.

It is good, I said, I am opening it; I am expanding it.

And I meant it.

I love you I texted Felix.
Lub u!!!!!! I texted Haruto.
Texting Isabella and Jackson, I love you guys.
I miss you.
I texted love you some forty-three times in the last few years.
I texted <3 some thirty-three times.
Lub u, eighteen times.
Miss you, thirty-eight.

She said your feed is all riots, plants, picnics, and poets.
It was an accusation.
She was noticing that I had got turnt.
And I said, my son, my son is in my feed too.
I didn't bother to argue the riot with her.

Still, oh that moment.
Turnt moment:

I was at the poetry reading and Mia didn't go. She was supposed to
    read too but she didn't. She said she wanted to see what happens.
    Then she texts I love you and I know then that Trader Joe's has
    been looted. All the wines out in the street.
Such sweet elixir, FOMO.
Then the rest of that night.
We quickly say good-byes after the reading, refuse the offer of going to
    drinks, careen from the reading to our home. One of us on twit-
    ter the entire time. Texting too. While we are driving, one of us at
    home runs out into the streets, towards the gas. I drive up and two
    of us get out of the car and I stay in the car and drive the few blocks
    home. My son has fallen asleep in the back. I am coughing in the
    car from the gas. He sleeps through it. I take him out and carry him
    up to bed. More texts. I love you, I text. Come by and get me when
    you are done.

Later that night, I go out again. Miguel stays home with Minjoon. I go
　　to a fight party; Marxist v. Nihilist. No one knows which is which.
　　Mohamed, my fighting teacher, fights. I miss it. I love you I text.
　　She texts back I'm high on being slugged; my eyes are swollen; I
　　lost; I'm turnt.
Standing outside, a woman gets kicked out of the club. The bouncer
　　tosses her out and into us. She is fucked up. And this feels awful to
　　her. Her arms wildly swinging indicate this awful feeling. It feels
　　awful to us. Another woman tries to help her and she slugs her. She
　　misses and the woman who she has tried to slug takes her, calms
　　her down. I hear her saying I love you, I love you over and over.
　　Later I will learn that she spent the entire night talking the woman
　　down. It's like that. When turnt, sometimes one needs to be held.
Still later, I stand on the street, outside my house and watch the
　　t-mobile get looted. A man tries to stop another man who has
　　his hammer at the ready in front of the window. The man who is
　　attempting to stop the hammer gets hit in the face with the butt
　　of the hammer. I decide to go to bed. It is 3 am. I text Nathan and
　　say I love you and I'll leave the key in the box for you. The march
　　continues on, Nathan continues on, turns left a block away and
　　then when Nathan texts me back I know the Whole Foods is looted
　　and they are all drinking champagne, dancing. All of them will get
　　a cold later.
Riot champagne becomes a term among us that winter.
I wasn't there but I was there too. My germs were there.
I too had that cold.

Is this poem too heroic?
I am sorry.
I worry it is.
Or I know it is.
We are turnt to mere vandals at moments. I'll admit it.
Every computer in that shop.
Every phone in that one.
Every car in that car lot.

I don't want it to be heroic but last night I turned the corner and Nor
   was there with her bike and when I saw her I said I love you and
   we walked down the street as each window was cracked. They got
   turnt. Eventually we disperse. I jog for a few minutes away and out
   of the kettle. We joke, circle back to watch a car burn. Oliver walks
   by. He is hurrying towards the dispersal. I love you we say to him as
   he heads off. The car burns. The fire truck arrives. As I stand there
   watching it, it is as if everyone I have ever texted I love you to walks
   by. I love you we call out to each other.
A group of women walk by the car and stop to take photographs. So
   much joy they have. They are laughing with such triumph. Selfies
   and all. Turnt.

This poem is true. I have texted I love you and its variations over
   and over.
Sometimes I barely knew you.
But the names are not true.
This is not a coterie poem.
Is it a milieu poem?
Can it be a movement poem?
I took all the names of this poem and never wrote them in.
There is no electronic record of them.
I found a list of the most popular baby names for various countries in
   2015, the year in which I am writing this poem. I made a list, one
   male and one female from each list. Then I alphabetized it. And I
   put these names in this poem one by one. I got to O.
But Olivia, Saanvi, Santiago, Seoyeon, Sofia, Yui, and Zeynep, I love
   you too.

ACKNOWLEDGEMENTS

"Transitory, Momentary" was written for SFMOMA's show *Mark di Suvero at Crissy Field*. Frank Smigiel and Kevin Killian co-organized a small chapbook of poetry, produced by Andrew Kenower and Lara Durback that included this work. Both "Brent Crude" and "Dynamic Positioning" were written for a series or readings that Cara Benson organized for Belladonna Collective and were published as a chapbook by Belladonna. "Tradition" appeared in *Trappe Tusind*. "Went Looking and Found Coyotes" appeared in *American Reader*, got reprinted in *Hi-Zero*. And "It's All Fucked, It's All Good" first appeared in *Lana Turner*. All this work is full of debts and thefts. "Calling You Here" riffs off of Butch Hancock's "If You Were a Bluebird." "Tradition" lists chemicals commonly found in breast milk. "It's All Fucked, It's All Good" steals some language from "The Rise and Fall of the Oakland Commune" (www.crimethinc.com/texts/recentfeatures/atc-oak.php). I'm sure there is more. Sorry if I haven't admitted it. Huge debts of friendships too. Too many to enumerate. Thanks especially though for the hand holding from Jasper Bernes, David Buuck, Melissa Buzzeo, Joshua Clover, Bill Luoma, Charles Weigl, and Stephanie Young.